OUR LIVING WORLD

Reptiles

By **Edward R. Ricciuti**

With Illustrations by William Simpson

Series Editor: Vincent Marteka
Introduction by John Behler, *New York Zoological Society*

A BLACKBIRCH PRESS BOOK

WOODBRIDGE, CONNECTICUT

Published by Blackbirch Press, Inc.
One Bradley Road, Suite 205
Woodbridge, CT 06525

©1993 Blackbirch Press, Inc.
First Edition

Printed in Canada

10 9 8 7 6 5 4 3 2

Editorial Director: Bruce Glassman
Editor: Geraldine C. Fox
Editorial Assistant: Michelle Spinelli
Design Director: Sonja Kalter
Production: Sandra Burr, Rudy Raccio

Library of Congress Cataloging-in-Publication Data

Ricciuti, Edward R.
    Reptiles / by Edward R. Ricciuti: introduction by John Behler—1st ed.
        p.   cm. — (Our living world)
    Includes bibliographical references and index.
    Summary: Explores the physical characteristics, senses, metabolism, reproduction, and growth of reptiles.
    ISBN 1-56711-047-9   ISBN 1-56711-063-0 (Trade)
    1. Reptiles—Juvenile literature. [1. Reptiles.] I. Title. II. Series.
QL644.2.R52   1993
597.9—dc20   93-19227
                                                                                          CIP
                                                                                          AC

Contents

What Does It Mean to Be "Alive"?

Introduction by John Behler,
New York Zoological Society

One summer morning, as I was walking through a beautiful field, I was inspired to think about what it really means to be "alive." Part of the answer, I came to realize, was right in front of my eyes.

The meadow was ablaze with color, packed with wildflowers at the height of their blooming season. A multitude of insects, warmed by the sun's early-morning rays, began to stir. Painted turtles sunned themselves on an old mossy log in a nearby pond. A pair of wood ducks whistled a call as they flew overhead, resting near a shagbark hickory on the other side of the pond.

As I wandered through this unspoiled habitat, I paused at a patch of milkweed to look for monarch-butterfly caterpillars, which depend on the milkweed's leaves for food. Indeed, the caterpillars were there, munching away. Soon these larvae would spin their cocoons, emerge as beautiful orange-and-black butterflies, and begin a fantastic 1,500-mile (2,400-kilometer) migration to wintering grounds in Mexico. It took biologists nearly one hundred years to unravel the life history of these butterflies. Watching them in the milkweed patch made me wonder how much more there is to know about these insects and all the other living organisms in just that one meadow.

The patterns of the natural world have often been likened to a spider's web, and for good reason. All life on Earth is interconnected in an elegant yet surprisingly simple design, and each living thing is an essential part of that design. To understand biology and the functions of living things, biologists have spent a lot of time looking at the differences among organisms. But in order to understand the very nature of living things, we must first understand what they have in common.

The butterfly larvae and the milkweed—and all animals and plants, for that matter—are made up of the same basic elements. These elements are obtained, used, and eliminated by every living thing in a series of chemical activities called metabolism.

Every molecule of every living tissue must contain carbon. During photosynthesis, green plants take in carbon dioxide from the atmosphere. Within their chlorophyll-filled leaves, in the presence of sunlight, the carbon dioxide is combined with water to form sugar—nature's most basic food. Animals need carbon, too. To grow and function, animals must eat plants or other animals that have fed on plants in order to obtain carbon. When plants and animals die, bacteria and fungi help to break down their tissues. This allows the carbon in plants and animals to be recycled. Indeed, the carbon in your body—and everyone else's body—may once have been inside a dinosaur, a giant redwood, or a monarch butterfly!

All life also needs nitrogen. Nitrogen is an essential component of protoplasm, the complex of chemicals that makes up living cells. Animals acquire nitrogen in the same manner as they acquire carbon dioxide: by eating plants or other animals that have eaten plants. Plants, however, must rely on nitrogen-fixing bacteria in the soil to absorb nitrogen from the atmosphere and convert it into proteins. These proteins are then absorbed from the soil by plant roots.

Living things start life as a single cell. The process by which cells grow and reproduce to become a specific organism—whether the organism is an oak tree or a whale—is controlled by two basic substances called deoxyribonucleic acid (DNA) and ribonucleic acid (RNA). These two chemicals are the building blocks of genes that determine how an organism looks, grows, and functions. Each organism has a unique pattern of DNA and RNA in its genes. This pattern determines all the characteristics of a living thing. Each species passes its unique pattern from generation to generation. Over many billions of years, a process involving genetic mutation and natural selection has allowed species to adapt to a constantly changing environment by evolving—changing genetic patterns. The living creatures we know today are the results of these adaptations.

Reproduction and growth are important to every species, since these are the processes by which new members of a species are created. If a species cannot reproduce and adapt, or if it cannot reproduce fast enough to replace those members that die, it will become extinct (no longer exist).

In recent years, biologists have learned a great deal about how living things function. But there is still much to learn about nature. With high-technology equipment and new information, exciting discoveries are being made every day. New insights and theories quickly make many biology textbooks obsolete. One thing, however, will forever remain certain: As living things, we share an amazing number of characteristics with other forms of life. As animals, our survival depends upon the food and functions provided by other animals and plants. As humans—who can understand the similarities and interdependence among living things—we cannot help but feel connected to the natural world, and we cannot forget our responsibility to protect it. It is only through looking at, and understanding, the rest of the natural world that we can truly appreciate what it means to be "alive."

1

Reptiles:
The Overview

People have lots of different ideas about reptiles. Many of these ideas, however, are not accurate. Snakes, for example, are not slimy, and most of them aren't really dangerous. Not all dinosaurs were huge, and not all lizards have legs.

Some reptiles, like the ancient dinosaurs, always fascinate people. Others, such as snakes, frighten many people. Reptiles are frequently thought of as "mysterious" creatures, but they are not any more mysterious than other types of animals. In fact, reptiles have a great deal in common with humans and other animals.

The Amazing Variety of Reptiles

There are four main groups, or orders, of reptiles, whose members include turtles; crocodiles, alligators, gavials, and caimans (crocodilians); lizards and

Opposite:
Red-sided garter snakes crowd together in a large nest. Many people have a fear of snakes that is based on a lack of knowledge about them.

snakes; and the tuatara. The tuatara is a species from New Zealand that looks like a lizard.

Scientists have identified about 6,200 kinds, or species, of reptiles. That's more than mammals and amphibians but not as many as birds and fishes. Thousands of other reptiles once existed, but they have become extinct (died out). Reptiles live in many different habitats. These include bone-dry deserts, fresh water, the sea, swamps, plains, and even city lots. They survive in most climates, but the greatest variety is in the tropics. Their numbers gradually decrease in the temperate (colder) zones. Only one species of lizard and one snake inhabit the Arctic. Neither species ranges much north of the Arctic Circle, however. Severe cold limits the range of reptiles because of their metabolism.

Reptiles come in all shapes and sizes. Some reptiles, such as the swift lizard, would fit into the palm of your hand. The British Virgin Island gecko, at an average length of 0.7 inches (18 millimeters) is the smallest reptile and can fit on the tip of your index finger. Other reptiles grow to very large sizes. The leatherback sea turtle, for example, can weigh about

Jelly Belly

The leatherback is the largest living species of turtle and can reach 8 feet (2 meters) long. After breeding in the warm waters of the Caribbean, leatherbacks feed on, and follow, jellyfish as they move west into the Atlantic. Because of their size, these turtles eat an incredible amount of jellyfish; young leatherbacks have been known to eat twice their weight in jellyfish every day. One leatherback that had drowned in a fishing net washed up on the shores of Harlech Bay in Wales. At 2,017 pounds (915 kilograms), this turtle was the biggest and one of the heaviest ever recorded.

Leatherback turtle

2,000 pounds (907 kilograms). The largest snakes are the anaconda and reticulated python. They can reach lengths of more than 25 feet (8 meters). The Komodo monitor, or "dragon," is the biggest lizard. A very large one can reach 12 feet (4 meters) and weigh 250 pounds (114 kilograms). The biggest crocodilian—and the biggest reptile—is the fish-eating Indian gavial, which is 30 feet (9 meters) long. The dwarf crocodile of Africa is only 3 feet (1 meter) from the tip of its snout to the end of its tail.

The worm lizard of southeastern North America is shaped like an earthworm. It lacks ear openings, legs, and eyes. Just like a worm, it spends much of its life underground, burrowing into the soil, searching for ants, termites, and worms.

Reptiles come in many shapes and sizes. The Komodo monitor lizard (*above, left*)—known also as the "dragon"—is the largest lizard. The dwarf crocodile (*above, middle*) grows to a length of 3 feet (1 meter) only and is one of the smallest crocodilians. And the North American worm lizard (*above, right*) is a member of the lizard family, but it looks and acts like an earthworm.

The Age of Reptiles

Reptiles were the first vertebrates (animals with backbones) that did not need to live in water for at least part of their lives. As descendants of amphibians, they have been on Earth approximately 300 million years. Mammals, in turn, developed, or evolved, from reptiles more than 200 million years ago.

During the Age of Reptiles, reptiles were the most common creatures on Earth. Many people think of

When Reptiles Ruled the Earth

About 300 million years ago, reptiles first roamed the planet and then became the most common animals on Earth. Some of the dinosaurs that lived during the Age of Reptiles are shown here. Today, scientists continue to uncover new facts about dinosaurs and the other reptiles that lived so long ago. As new discoveries are made, new theories about dinosaurs are discussed. Were they all gigantic monsters with little intelligence? Were they clumsy and slow, or were there some that were actually swift and graceful? How did they become extinct?

Recent studies have revealed some fascinating new information about dinosaurs. High-tech computers and space-age analyzing tools have uncovered evidence from fossilized (preserved in stone) bones, dinosaur nests, eggs, and footprints. In 1993, a new dinosaur species from Mongolia was found. It was a turkey-sized flightless bird called *Mononychus* that had feathers and a bone structure that was part bird and part dinosaur. Now many scientists believe that *Tyrannosaurus rex* is more closely related to birds than to any other kind of dinosaur!

11

the Age of Reptiles only in terms of dinosaurs, but lots of other reptiles lived during that time. Giant lizards, such as *Tylosaurus*, swam in the sea. Huge flying reptiles, the size of small airplanes, glided through the air. Crocodiles, big enough to eat some dinosaurs, lurked in rivers.

But dinosaurs, which have since died out, were most numerous. They came in all shapes and sizes. Some weighed 50 tons (45 metric tons) and were more than 100 feet (31 meters) long. Others were not much bigger than chickens. Most fell somewhere in between in size.

People used to think of dinosaurs as "dumb brutes," but now many scientists believe that a large number of them were actually very intelligent. Some lived in herds, and many spent a great deal of time protecting and caring for their young. The dinosaurs were active, complex animals.

No one knows exactly why the dinosaurs died out. Many scientists believe that a huge object from space, such as a giant meteor, hit the Earth and caused vast environmental changes. The impact released so much dust that it formed a thick layer in the atmosphere that blocked out the sun. With less light or heat, many species of plants and animals died out.

The Age of Reptiles is long gone, but the reptiles that remain today are reminders of the time when their kind ruled the Earth. At certain places, at certain times of the year, it is easy to be reminded of the ties between modern reptiles and their ancient relatives. During the spring, deep in the Okefenokee Swamp of Georgia, the ground rumbles to the roaring grunts of male alligators. It is mating season, and the alligators bellow to stake out territories and attract females. The sound of a male alligator calling in the darkness of the great swamp is at the same time eerie

DID YOU KNOW

Gator-Aid

Do you know the difference between an alligator and a crocodile? Here's how you can tell them apart. An alligator's snout is broad and somewhat rounded. A crocodile's snout is long and narrow. When an alligator's mouth is shut, only its upper teeth are visible. When a crocodile's mouth is closed, you can see some of both the upper and lower teeth—especially the big fourth tooth on each side of its lower jaw.

Reptiles: The Overview

and awesome. The bellowing reminds us that, while the days of greatness are vanished for the reptiles, they still do many of the things that their ancestors did hundreds of millions of years ago.

Reptile Features

The first reptiles were not that much different from their amphibian ancestors. With time, however, they evolved and differed more. The reptiles on Earth today all share a number of important features.

Backbones Like humans and other vertebrates, reptiles have a bony skeleton that supports the body. Muscles are anchored to the skeleton. The center-piece of the skeleton is a backbone, which runs down the center of the back, just as yours does. Inside the backbone is the spinal cord, which contains nerves that are linked to the brain. Nerves branch out from the spinal cord to other parts of the body. The backbone is made up of a number of smaller bones called vertebrae.

Scales and scutes A reptile's body is covered with scales that are composed mostly of a hard material similar to that of human fingernails.

The scales of crocodilians and a turtle's shell are reinforced with plates of bone. They are called scutes.

The scales of a snake feel smooth, but many other reptiles have rough or horny scales. Scales protect a

Ocean Motion: Swimming Snakes

About 50 kinds of snakes live in the tropical seas. A sea snake has a tail that is flattened top to bottom, like an oar. It uses its tail to swim. The nostrils of a sea snake are on top of its snout. They can be closed by valves when the snake is underwater. Sea snakes eat eels and other fishes. They are venomous (poisonous), but they do not often attack swimmers.

Banded sea snake

Reptile skin is made up of a combination of scales and scutes. Scales are small and hard but flexible, like human fingernails. Scutes are bone-like and inflexible. The skin of an Indian python, shown here, feels smooth, but it is really made of overlapping scales that protect the animal's outer body.

reptile's skin and, if they are large and sharp, they can ward off predators. Scales also prevent a reptile from losing too much moisture. This is particularly important for reptiles that live in the desert.

Teeth Most reptiles have teeth, although turtles do not. Turtles cut up food with the sharp edges of their horny beaks. As a rule, reptiles shed their teeth and grow new ones several times during their lifetimes. Reptile teeth do not fall out all at once. As teeth are shed, other teeth grow in on each side of the mouth.

The teeth in the mouths of most reptiles all have similar shapes—many are the same size. The fangs of venomous snakes are an exception. They are long, and they are grooved, or channeled, to carry their venom.

Reptile teeth are best adapted to grabbing food and, in many cases, cutting it up. Reptiles swallow food whole or in chunks and do not chew the way mammals do. A mammal has teeth of many different types that perform various jobs, such as cutting and chewing. Chewing breaks down food so it is digested more efficiently. This is why mammals get more energy out of their food than reptiles.

Cold-bloodedness Reptiles cannot stand the cold, because they do not produce very much body heat. (Some snakes can produce a little heat.) Reptiles are cold-blooded; that is, their body temperature

Slithering Along: Snakes and Travel

Some snakes have 300 vertebrae. (You have 33.) Each vertebra is attached to a pair of ribs. A ball and a socket join the vertebrae. This arrangement allows the snake to coil and twist.

Twisting and coiling are the keys to a snake's movement. Its belly is covered with wide scales that overlap backward. Each scale is attached by muscles to a pair of ribs. As the snake moves, the scales catch on the surface underneath, and the muscles move the snake ahead.

Snakes travel in four ways. One way is to travel forward by curving the body into an S shape. Each time it curves, the snake uses the ground to shove itself ahead. The sidewinder rattlesnake and some other desert snakes throw their bodies sideways in an S shape, which is a good way to travel in the sand.

If the ground, or another surface, is too smooth, a snake uses a different method for movement. It moves the forward part of its body ahead until it comes into contact with something; then it pulls the rest of its body along. The movement of the body is like that of the bellows in an accordion.

Still another way that snakes move is to simply creep straight ahead, using the belly scales like the treads of a combat tank to grip the ground for traction and pull the snake forward.

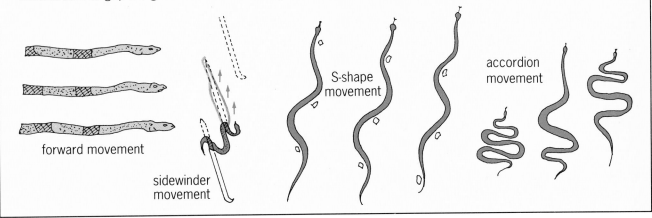

forward movement

sidewinder movement

S-shape movement

accordion movement

is determined by the temperature of their surroundings. A cold lizard, for example, must bask in the sun to warm up. If the outside temperature is too hot, the lizard must get under cover to cool down.

The shelled egg Most reptiles develop in eggs. They were the first animals to have a shelled egg. The tough, leathery shell holds in fluids, which nourish the reptile embryo within the egg and keep it moist. A shelled egg was a big step in the development of vertebrate life. It enabled reptiles to reproduce on land, which, in turn, enabled them to spread over all the Earth's continents, except Antarctica.

The Senses:
How Reptiles React

The chameleon of Africa is a lizard that can look backward with one eye and forward with the other. Its huge eyes bulge like rounded cones from each side of its head. Each of its eyelids covers all the eyeball but the pupil. The chameleon can move each eye independently. The eyeball rotates as if it were on a swivel and has a field of vision of a half-circle. A chameleon can thus see all the way around itself.

When a chameleon's eyes are operating independently, the animal has no depth perception, so it can't judge distances well. When both eyes are focusing on something, however, the chameleon sees keenly in three dimensions and can make accurate estimates of distance. This visual ability helps a chameleon catch insects and spiders with its long tongue. Once it pinpoints the distance to its target, the chameleon shoots out its tongue, which can be longer than its

Opposite:
In order to survive, all living things must be able to react well to their surroundings. Chameleons have special eyes that can move independently of each other. This allows chameleons to see all the way around themselves and to better focus on their prey.

Chameleons have tongues that are as long as their bodies. Their tongues are hollow and are sticky at the tip. When a chameleon focuses on its prey, it shoots its tongue out at lightning speed and grabs its victim. A chameleon can hit a target more than 1 foot (0.3 meter) away with incredible accuracy. After the chameleon has hit its victim, it coils its tongue back into its mouth.

body. And the chameleon can often be deadly accurate. Chameleons are capable of hitting insects that are 1 foot (0.3 meter) or more away, and they do it in a flash—almost too fast for anyone to see.

Vision is just one of the senses that give a reptile—and most other living things—information about what is going on in the environment. Eyes and other sense organs detect changes in surroundings. Any change in the environment that is detected by the sense organs of a living thing is called a stimulus. Stimuli continually bombard the sense organs of any creature that is alive.

The Senses: How Reptiles React

The time between a stimulus and response can be incredibly fast—just an instant. (Think about how quickly you turn around when someone behind you calls your name.) Stimuli can also be gradual. The gradual decrease in temperatures in the fall, for instance, sends rattlesnakes to dens, where they will rest quietly for the winter.

Like many other animals, reptiles rely on sight, hearing, smell, and touch. They do not appear to have a very developed sense of taste, however.

How Reptiles See

Sight is the sense that is most commonly used among reptiles, and most reptiles have very keen eyesight.

Focusing The eye of a reptile, like that of any vertebrate, works much like a camera. Light enters the eye through the lens. The amount of light that enters the lens is controlled by the iris. In dim situations, the iris widens to let more light enter the lens. In bright light, the iris contracts to reduce the light to the lens. Behind the eyeball is a coating called the retina. It is the eye's "film." When light falls on the retina, it registers an image. The optic nerve then sends the image to the brain, where it is "developed" into a "picture."

The lens of a vertebrate's eye is flexible, and it changes shape so as to focus on objects at different distances. There are both similarities and differences in the ways that human and reptile lenses focus. Both ways are controlled by similar muscles. When the muscles in your eye relax, the lens flattens, which allows the eye to focus on objects at a distance. When your eye muscles contract, the lens bulges for close-up viewing. By comparison, when the muscles in the eye of a lizard, for example, contract, they press against the perimeter of the lens. The pressure rounds

Focus-Pocus

A chameleon can move its eyes independently of each other and has an exceptionally wide field of vision. When the chameleon sees prey, it focuses one eye on the prey and uses the other eye to help it move toward the animal. Once it is close enough to its intended victim, the chameleon focuses both eyes on the prey for binocular vision. This kind of vision provides depth and dimension most accurately for pouncing.

A snake's lens works differently from that of other reptiles. When a snake's eye focuses on something nearby, muscles push the lens forward rather than bend it into a different shape. For distance, the lens moves backward in the eye.

The primitive tuatara has a third "eye." The tuatara looks like a lizard—its two normal eyes are in the same place as a lizard's. But between the two eyes, just under the skin on top of the tuatara's head, is a third "eye." It is a structure that, like an eye, is sensitive to light. A few lizards have a similar structure. Scientists do not believe that the third eye can really see, but some ancient reptiles may have used this third eye for extra vision.

19

Many reptiles rely heavily on their eyesight for survival. Although all reptile eyes work in much the same way on the inside, they vary in structure on the outside. The rat snake (*top*), like other snakes, for example, does not have movable eyelids. The tokay gecko (*bottom*), like most lizards, has an eyelid that can blink.

the lens to better focus on close objects. When the muscles relax, the lens flattens for focusing on objects at a distance.

Eyelids Most reptiles have two eyelids and can blink. Blinking is a way to keep the eyes clean. Most also have an organ, the nictitating membrane, which further protects the eye. This membrane is clear, and when it moves across the eye, it sweeps away dirt particles. A reptile can see through its nictitating membrane. The membrane covers an alligator's eye when it submerges itself in the water, allowing it to see clearly underwater. The eye of a snake lacks movable eyelids, so the animal can't blink. Instead, a clear scale covers and protects the eye.

Color vision Vertebrate eyes have vision cells called rods and cones, which are named for their shapes. Rods are very sensitive to light. They help an animal see in dim light. An animal that is active at night, such as the alligator, has many rods in its eyes. Cones work best in bright light. A chameleon, active during the day, has a larger number of cones in its eyes than does an alligator.

Cones are also the key to seeing colors. Many reptiles, such as lizards and turtles, have color vision. Alligators, however, probably lack the ability to see color. Many nocturnal animals (those active at night) lack color vision. Colors are hard to detect at night, and it is more important for nocturnal animals to pick out shapes and movement in the darkness.

Glow Gators

In many parts of the United States, alligators are common enough to be hunted legally during special times of the year. Their hides are valuable for use in clothing and accessories. Not long ago, alligators were on the list of endangered species. Recently, alligator poachers have killed the animals in violation of wildlife regulations. One way poachers do this is to search for alligators at night with a flashlight. They take advantage of an area of the alligator's eye called the tapetum.

The tapetum is a layer of cells behind the retina that mirrors light passing through the retina. As a result, the retina picks up light a second time that it otherwise would have lost. The tapetum is an advantage for an animal like the alligator, which is active at night, because it helps the alligator to see better in darkness.

When a flashlight is shone into an alligator's eyes after dark and then turned off, the tapetum in the alligator's eyes glows like coals. This makes alligators easy targets for poachers, who shoot at the glowing eyes.

Glowing alligator eyes

How Reptiles Hear

The ear of most reptiles is somewhat similar to that of birds—that's because birds evolved from reptiles. Like birds, reptiles do not have a visible outer ear. Many reptiles—lizards, for example—have an ear-drum that is visible on the outside of the head. Sound comes from vibrations that travel in the form of energy waves through matter, such as air or water. An eardrum picks up sound vibrations, which are then sent as messages to the brain. As in birds, the vibrations are transmitted through a single bone, called the stapes, behind the eardrum. The vibrations travel through the bone to a tube-like structure in the inner ear that is filled with fluid. As the vibrations pass through the fluid, they are picked up by nerve cells as stimuli. The vibrations are then changed into nerve signals and are sent to the brain, where they are interpreted as sound.

Skinks, like most lizards, have a visible eardrum on each side of their head. The reptile eardrum is much like a human one; it picks up sound as vibration and transmits signals as messages to the brain.

Tongue-Tied

Have you ever wondered why a snake or a lizard constantly flicks its tongue in the air? It's not to try to look scary. The forked tongue is actually picking up scent particles in the air and on the ground. As it retracts, the tongue transfers these scents to cells in the roof of the reptile's mouth located in what is called the Jacobson's organ. By helping the animal to "smell" or "taste" scents, this organ allows it to trail prey, sample food, detect enemies, and find a mate.

Since snakes do not have eardrums, they cannot hear—at least not in the way humans or most other vertebrates do. However, the bones in a snake's lower jaw can pick up vibrations from the ground.

A reptile's jaw joint is formed by the meeting of two bones, the articular and the quadrate. Vibrations travel from the ground through the snake's lower jaw. From there, the vibrations pass through the articular bone to the quadrate bone and then to the stapes, which transmits the vibrations to the inner ear. The inner ear then sends a signal to the brain, which translates the signals as sound.

Smell and Touch

Reptiles sense odors much the way humans do. Molecules of scent-carrying chemicals in the air enter the nose. Nerve cells then pick up the scents—which are stimuli—and relay the information to the brain as nerve messages, which register as smell.

Reptiles also smell with a structure called the Jacobson's organ. This organ is most highly developed in lizards and snakes. In the roof of a lizard's

Super Snake Pit

Rattlesnake

Some snakes have an extra sense that helps them find prey. The rattlesnake, for example, can sense the heat given off by the body of a bird or mammal. (Birds and mammals produce a good deal of heat within their bodies.) Between each eye and nostril of the rattlesnake is a pit that contains heat-sensing nerve cells. Some snakes also have these cells on their lips.

Heat, like light, is given off in the form of energy waves. The vertebrate eye cannot see heat energy, but special electronic devices can. There are special cameras—called infrared cameras—that can register an image of heat given off by a body or other object. A rattlesnake's pit can also pick up the heat produced by an animal such as a mouse. Using this unique sense, a snake can find a mouse in complete darkness.

Scientists have blindfolded rattlesnakes to test their heat-seeking abilities. When a cold light bulb is waved before a blindfolded rattlesnake, the animal doesn't strike. But it does strike at a warm bulb. And its strike is right on target. Because they have this special organ, rattlesnakes and their relatives are commonly known as pit vipers.

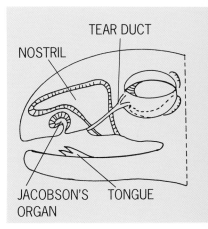

Snakes and lizards flick their tongues in the air to pick up scents. Cells in their tongues bring scent information into the mouth, where it is sensed by the Jacobson's organ.

TEAR DUCT
NOSTRIL
JACOBSON'S ORGAN
TONGUE

mouth is an opening that leads to two chambers, which are lined with odor-sensitive cells. These two chambers open through the roof of the mouth. Snakes and some lizards constantly flick their forked tongues in the air. Their tongues bring scented particles from the air or ground to the opening of the Jacobson's organ, where cells inside the chambers register the scent. Because of its sensitivity, the Jacobson's organ is a big help to a reptile in finding food.

Touch is a basic and very important sense and was probably the first sense possessed by living things. An amoeba, for example, cannot hear, see, smell, or taste, but it reacts when it touches another object. If the object is food, the amoeba will engulf it. If it is not food, the amoeba will withdraw.

Animals sense touch through the action of nerve cells in the outer coverings of their bodies. The outer layer of an animal body is usually some form of skin. Reptiles have skin, but most of it is not as sensitive to touch as that of a human or other mammal. Scales and scutes reduce the reptile's sensitivity.

The Senses: How Reptiles React

Metabolism: How Reptiles Function

Reptiles feed on a very wide variety of things. Box turtles eat insects, leaves, and berries. Rattlesnakes feed mostly on small mammals. Marine iguanas, which are large lizards, eat seaweeds. For a reptile, as for any other living organism, food is the fuel that enables the body to function. The body uses food to make the energy an organism needs to grow and stay alive. The basic processes of obtaining, digesting, and utilizing food are called metabolism. Before metabolism can begin, living things must obtain food from somewhere. Animals rely on their senses to locate food. Once an animal has found food, it will eat and digest it. During digestion, the food is broken down into substances that can be used and stored in the body.

These digested substances combine with oxygen, releasing energy. This is the energy that the body uses to function. (The same thing happens when wood burns. Light and heat energy are released when oxygen combines with substances in the wood.) Reptiles, like birds and mammals, get oxygen by breathing the air around them. This is a part of a process called respiration.

The ashes left over after a wood fire are the material from the logs that were not fully converted to light and heat. This ash is the "waste" left over after the energy has been released. Similarly, not all food that an animal consumes is turned into energy. In this case, undigested food is the waste.

Many chemical processes in the body must interact in a delicate balance to keep an organism's metabolism working properly. As long as metabolism continues properly, an organism will remain healthy. When metabolism breaks down, however, an organism loses energy, and necessary activities, such as getting food, slow down. If the breakdown is bad enough, the organism dies.

One factor that separates birds and mammals from reptiles is their metabolic rate. A bird's or a mammal's metabolism operates at a much higher rate than does a reptile's. Birds and mammals need a great deal of energy to produce their own body heat. In

The Shell Game

Matamata turtle

A turtle looks like a turtle, right? Not the matamata turtle of South America. Its flat shell is studded with knobby points and coated with algae. Its head is also flat, shaped like a big leaf, and it is covered with warts and bumps. When the matamata lies on the bottom of the water, it looks like a pile of leaves and other vegetation. If a fish comes near, the matamata opens its huge mouth and sucks in a rush of water—if it is successful, the fish is pulled in, too.

The shape of the matamata and its feeding behavior are traits that enable it to survive. Such traits are called adaptations. Adaptations occur by chance as a species evolves, or changes over very long periods of time. Species that have adaptations suited to their environment will survive. Those that do not adapt to their environment will eventually vanish, or become extinct.

Anatomy of a Reptile

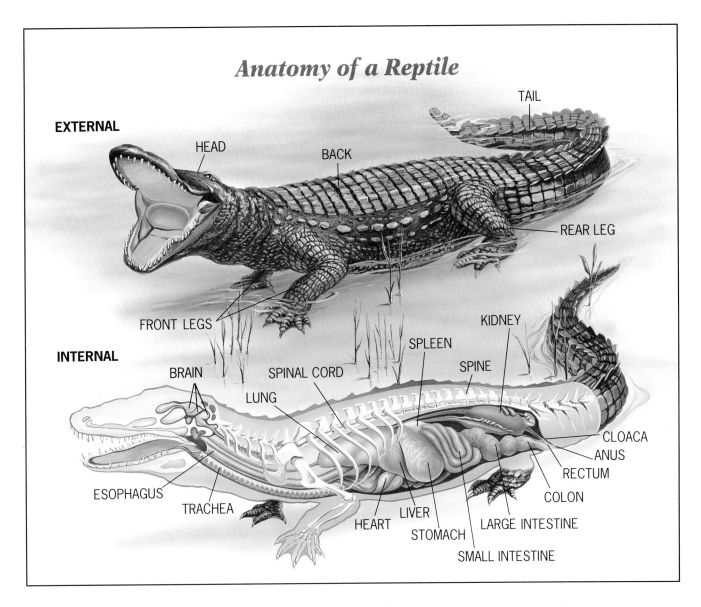

EXTERNAL

TAIL

HEAD

BACK

REAR LEG

FRONT LEGS

INTERNAL

BRAIN

SPINAL CORD

SPLEEN

KIDNEY

SPINE

LUNG

CLOACA

ANUS

RECTUM

COLON

ESOPHAGUS

TRACHEA

HEART

LIVER

LARGE INTESTINE

STOMACH

SMALL INTESTINE

order to get enough fuel, birds and mammals must eat much more frequently than reptiles. Some medium-size boa constrictors can get by on a rat or two a week. Others may require a rat only every other week.

Reptiles take most of their body heat from their surroundings. Almost all the energy they get from food, therefore, can be used for other processes, such as growth and movement. That is how reptiles can function on relatively little energy.

When a reptile's surroundings increase its body temperature, however, its rate of metabolism rises. Then the reptile needs additional food and oxygen because it is also more active. A snake, for example, moves more on a warm day than it does on a cool one.

Metabolism: How Reptiles Function

Not in the Mood for Food

A scientific experiment showed the great difference between the metabolism of reptiles and that of warm-blooded animals. Researchers measured the amount of fish and meat that seven 100-pound (45-kilogram) alligators had eaten in a year. They found that, together, it equaled the amount of food eaten during the same time period by just one 95-pound (43-kilogram) dog.

Tuataras are the last remaining species of a group of primitive reptiles. Because they inhabit the rocky coasts of New Zealand, tuataras eat seabird eggs and nestlings, snails, earthworms, and crickets.

What Reptiles Eat

Some reptiles eat plants, but most of them eat other animals—including other reptiles.

The tuatara, which looks like a big lizard, is the last surviving species of a group of primitive reptiles that vanished before the dinosaurs died out. It lives on islands along the coast of New Zealand. Although it eats mostly crickets, sometimes it feeds on seabird eggs and nestlings, earthworms, and snails.

Lizards are mainly insect-eaters. In the desert of Australia lives the moloch lizard, which is only about 8 inches (20 centimeters) long and looks like a tiny dragon. Sharp spines cover its body, but it is not dangerous, except to ants. The moloch uses its broad, thick tongue to catch ants, which can number more than 1,000 for a normal meal.

The little green anole lizard, which lives in the southwestern United States, eats mostly insects and spiders. It captures some with its sticky tongue, but it is also fast enough to grab an insect in its jaws.

The four-inch (10-centimeter) collared lizard of the southwestern United States is a ferocious critter. It eats both insects and other lizards. Quick and nimble, it can run on its rear legs alone, rushing and seizing prey in its strong jaws. The huge Komodo monitor lizard, or "dragon," also rushes at its prey. Its

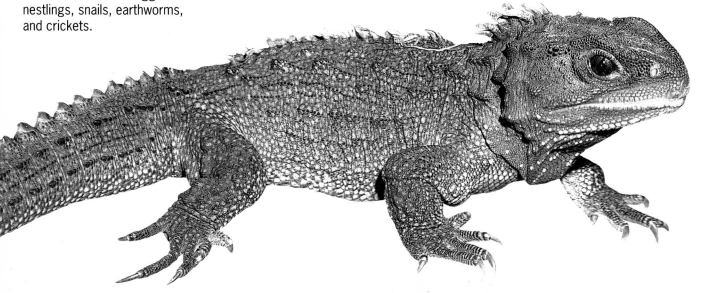

prey, however, are much larger than animals eaten by the collared lizard. The Komodo monitor eats pigs and goats and has even killed a few people for food.

The water habitats of American alligators and snapping turtles offer these reptiles a wide variety of animals on which to feed—water birds, snails, crabs, crayfishes, fishes, and frogs.

Different snakes catch food in different ways. The indigo snake of the southeastern United States overpowers and pins down rats, birds, and other small animals. The boa constrictor catches mammals and birds by striking with its mouth open and seizing the prey in its teeth. Quick as a flash, the boa wraps its muscular body around its victim and tightens, or constricts. The pressure stops the prey's lungs and heart and causes death. The small brown snake, which is about the size of a pencil, seizes insects and earthworms in its jaws.

Some snakes kill prey with poison, or venom. Venom is produced in glands similar to those that make saliva in humans. All snakes have these glands,

An alligator feeds on some prey in a swamp. Because reptiles are cold-blooded instead of warm-blooded (like mammals), they require much less energy to function. They also have a much slower rate of metabolism, which means that they need much less food to survive.

Metabolism: How Reptiles Function

Some snakes, like this emerald tree boa, kill their prey by suffocation. Boa constrictors wrap their bodies around their victims and squeeze so tightly that the lungs and heart of their prey stop working.

Pit Viper Venom and Fangs

2.
Venom passes through a tube in the fang.

3.
Venom enters prey through a hole in the tip of the fang.

1.
Venom sac produces poison.

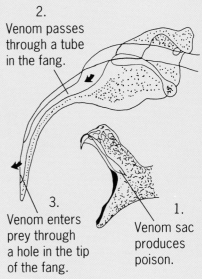

but only about 200 of the approximately 3,000 different kinds of snakes produce venom. Snakes that produce their own poison are called venomous snakes. Their glands channel venom to two fangs—one on each side of the snake's upper jaw. When a snake bites, venom enters the victim's body.

Most snake venoms are powerful poisons that can cause death almost instantly. Others cause a slow, painful death. The venom of the diamondback rattlesnake attacks the red blood cells and nervous system of its prey. The venom of the Australian death adder attacks the respiratory system. Two North American lizards, the Gila monster and Mexican beaded lizard, are also venomous.

Digesting Food

Digestion is the process by which a living thing breaks down food for use by the body. A reptile's digestive system is similar to that of a human. Both systems have a tube that leads from the mouth to the stomach. In the stomach, glands secrete digestive juices that contain chemicals called enzymes, which break the

About 200 kinds of snakes produce their own venom. These snakes inject a powerful poison through their hollow front fangs into the bodies of their prey.

DID YOU KNOW

Fang-tastic

Pit vipers are the most advanced venomous snakes. Their fangs are hollow and long, up to 1 inch (3 centimeters). When not in use, the fangs lie folded back in the jaw. As a pit viper strikes, the fangs pivot forward and up to stab the victim almost horizontally (straight forward). As the fangs penetrate, they inject venom.

Metabolism: How Reptiles Function

Big Mouth

An egg-eating snake swallows a quail egg whole.

Many snakes kill their prey by strangulation or suffocation. Once the prey is dead, a snake will usually swallow its victim whole. A snake can swallow animals much larger than its head. A python that is 25 feet (8 meters) long can swallow an animal the size of a German Shepherd. A garter snake no bigger around than a man's finger can swallow a toad.

A snake's jaw and skin are especially adapted to swallowing large items. The lower jaw of a snake is flexible and is hinged at the rear so it can drop far down. Moreover, each side of the jaw can move on its own, so a snake can open its mouth very wide. A snake's teeth point toward the rear. This helps to work food down the snake's throat. When a snake swallows large prey, its ribs expand. They can do this because they are not joined in front (as yours are, by a breastbone). The skin of a snake also helps in eating creatures. It stretches so that the body can bulge after the snake swallows a large meal.

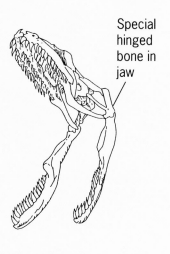

Special hinged bone in jaw

food down into simpler elements. In humans, chewing starts the breakdown of food in the mouth. Reptiles, however, can't chew, so they need strong digestive juices. A snake's digestive enzymes are so strong that it can digest even bones.

From the stomach, broken-down food goes to the small intestine for further digestion. Then it combines with water and enters the bloodstream. The blood then distributes the food molecules to the cells of the body.

Metabolism: How Reptiles Function

Breathing

Breathing is a constant exchange of gases between a living organism and the atmosphere. This exchange usually involves breathing in to obtain oxygen and then breathing out to rid the body of carbon dioxide. Reptiles breathe much the way many other animals do. Air carrying oxygen enters the nostrils and travels to the lungs through a tube called the windpipe. The lungs contain many small blood vessels with thin walls. In the lungs, oxygen passes into the blood, which carries it to the heart. The heart then sends the oxygen-rich blood to the tissues and organs throughout the rest of the body.

When a body's cells burn food to make energy, carbon dioxide waste is created. This waste is carried to the lungs by blood that needs to be reoxygenated. As oxygen enters the blood in the lungs, the carbon dioxide escapes. It is then expelled from the lungs when an animal breathes out, or exhales.

Removing Wastes

Metabolism in living things creates waste. Because all living organisms must metabolize in order to survive, they create and remove bodily wastes as well. Undigested food matter, which is stored in the large intestine, leaves the body through the anus. In reptiles, the anus opens at a compartment called the cloaca. A tube leading from the kidneys also opens at the cloaca, and urine passes through it. By producing urine, the kidneys help the body to remove nitrogen—metabolic waste—from the blood. Most reptiles do not have liquid urine as humans do. They produce solid or semisolid urine, which helps the body to conserve water. Water conservation is very important for reptiles that must survive in dry habitats, such as deserts.

DID YOU KNOW

Egg-cellent

Two types of tropical snakes swallow birds' eggs whole. These snakes have bones projecting from their vertebrae that come into the throat to break egg shells. The snakes eat the contents of an egg and then bring the broken shell back up into their mouths before they spit it out.

Metabolism: How Reptiles Function

The Circulatory System

Blood circulates through the body of an animal by means of a system of tubes called capillaries, veins, and arteries. The pump that moves the blood is the heart. Most reptiles have a heart with three chambers: a right atrium, a left atrium, and a ventricle. Crocodiles, alligators, and their relatives have a heart with four chambers, just like birds, humans, and other mammals. Their ventricle is divided into a right and a left subchamber.

One system of veins takes a reptile's blood, which is carrying oxygen from the lungs, and brings it to the left atrium of the heart. From the left atrium, the blood goes to the ventricle. A large artery then carries the blood from the ventricle to all the parts of the reptile's body.

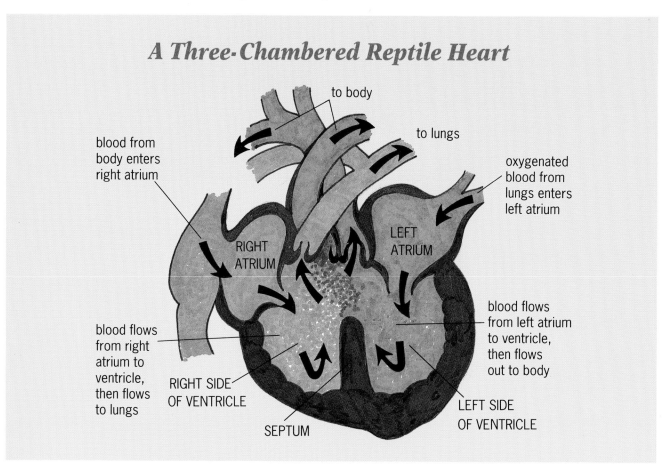

A Three-Chambered Reptile Heart

to body

to lungs

blood from body enters right atrium

oxygenated blood from lungs enters left atrium

RIGHT ATRIUM

LEFT ATRIUM

blood flows from right atrium to ventricle, then flows to lungs

blood flows from left atrium to ventricle, then flows out to body

RIGHT SIDE OF VENTRICLE

SEPTUM

LEFT SIDE OF VENTRICLE

In Cold Blood

Because reptiles are cold-blooded, they are greatly affected by the temperature of their environment. To cope with this, reptiles have certain physical and behavioral adaptations that keep them from getting too hot or too cold as the temperature of their surroundings changes.

The chuckwalla, a small lizard that lives in the hot deserts of North America, spends the cool desert night in a burrow because temperatures underground are more stable than those above ground and because the earth retains some of the day's heat. When the sun comes up, the chuckwalla emerges. To warm up, it basks in the sun, placing its body perpendicular to the sun's rays. This way, it exposes the maximum amount of its body surface to the warmth. The chuckwalla's skin has color cells that contain pigments. While the animal is basking, the black pigment in these cells expands to absorb as much sunlight as possible.

If the day gets too hot for the chuckwalla, the black pigment shrinks, and lighter pigments—which reflect sunlight—are exposed. If its body gets too hot, the chuckwalla creeps under a rock or seeks shade under a bush. Sometimes it even needs to return to its burrow until the temperature outside drops.

Most other reptiles have similar adaptations for coping with temperature. During the cold northern winter, reptiles remain in caves and burrows for long periods of time. Their metabolism slows down a lot. They don't need much oxygen or food, and they act as if they were in a deep sleep. This slowed-down state is called hibernation. When spring arrives, bringing with it warmer temperatures, reptiles slowly become active again.

Blood from which oxygen has been removed is brought back to the heart by another system of veins. The deoxygenated, or "spent," blood enters the right atrium, and then the ventricle. With the pumping of the heart, another large artery sends this "spent" blood to the lungs for another dose of oxygen.

Both types of blood may sometimes mix a little bit in the ventricle. This doesn't occur in crocodiles, humans, or other animals with four-chambered hearts, because their ventricle has two chambers. The left chamber pumps oxygen-rich blood through the body, and the right pumps blood that needs to get oxygen from the lungs.

Metabolism: How Reptiles Function

4

Reproduction and Growth

 Darkness cloaks the sands of Jupiter Beach, Florida. Over the Atlantic, heat lightning flashes in the sky. The surf crashes on the shore. A large humped form appears in the waves, several feet off the beach. Moonlight reflects on a giant rough shell. A massive head rears above the water as the form slowly moves toward the beach. Four broad flippers drag it up to the sand. An Atlantic loggerhead sea turtle weighing more than 200 pounds (91 kilograms) has come to lay her eggs in the sand.

Sea turtles mate in the water. Once their eggs are fertilized, the females go ashore to lay them in the very same beaches where they themselves hatched. Two months later, young turtles hatch from the eggs and go out to sea.

Creating new members of a species is one of the most important functions carried out by any living

Opposite:
Two green turtles mate in the warm waters of the Pacific Ocean. Reproducing new members of a species is one of the most important functions of any living thing.

thing. A species can continue to exist only by creating enough new members to make up for those lost to death. The process by which a species creates members of its own kind is called reproduction.

Getting Ready to Mate

Like the majority of animals, most reptiles require both a male and a female to mate. Reptiles—and many other animals—mate only at certain times of the year. In temperate climates, such as North America, mating may take place just once during a year, usually in the spring. Some reptiles, like the green turtle, mate only once every two or three years.

As a reptile gets ready to mate, changes take place in its body. These changes are caused by chemicals called hormones. Outside influences, such as more hours of sunlight and warmer temperatures, cause a reptile's body to produce hormones that prepare it for mating. Sex cells are produced in the body. Female sex cells are eggs; male sex cells are sperm. Sometimes there are also outward changes in the reptile's body, usually in the male. Many male lizards become very colorful when it is time to mate. Colorful displays by males during mating season are common throughout the natural world. Scientists have found that lots of female animals are attracted to bright colors, especially red.

Meeting a Mate

Like other animals, reptiles have many ways to meet and attract a mate. The males usually advertise that they are ready to mate. Male alligators do this by roaring, just as a male robin sings or a male gorilla beats its chest.

Like the song of a male bird, the roar of a bull (male) alligator is also a signal to other males that warns them to stay away. Color can act as the same kind of warning, as well as a means of attracting females. The male anole lizard, for example, can fan out the skin of his throat. During mating season, the fan is brightly colored, and the raised fan signals other males to keep clear. The display also tells females that the male is ready to mate.

Two male rattlesnakes will compete for a mate with a special "dance." They twist and turn around each other with their heads reared as they press against each other and push. It looks like a fight, but neither snake gets hurt.

Mating

The opening of the reptile's reproductive system is the cloaca, which is usually located under the base of the tail. The male's sexual organ is within his cloaca and is shaped like a tube. Male lizards and snakes have a pair of sexual organs that are used one at a time. When the male mates, the organ turns inside out to expose a groove that runs along it. When the organ is inserted into the female's cloaca, sperm cells travel through the tube to

The male anole lizard uses his throat to attract females. He puffs out his bright-red throat sac and walks around displaying the giant bulge. An inflated throat sac is also a sign of aggression and a warning to other males in the area to stay away.

A loggerhead turtle deposits her eggs in the sand of a beach in South Africa. A female may lay several batches of eggs in one season, laying an average of 120 eggs each time.

the inside of the female's body. There sperm fertilize the egg cells. A developing young reptile, called an embryo, then grows within the egg.

Nesting and Development

The eggs of some lizards and snakes stay in the female until the young hatch. Most reptiles, however, hatch from an egg after it has been laid in a nest by the female. Many female reptiles work hard to make nests for their eggs.

Nesting season for the female loggerhead turtle comes once every couple of years. She may lay several batches of eggs in a season—an average of 120 eggs each time. This may sound like a lot, but from each batch only a few young survive.

The loggerhead turtle places her eggs in a hole that she digs on the beach in the sand with her hind flippers. The nest must be above the high-tide mark. If it isn't, the eggs may be washed away. After laying her eggs, the female covers them with sand and returns to the water.

When the young turtles hatch in two months, they are about the size of a half dollar and look like tiny copies of their parents. This is not the case for most amphibians and fishes, which begin life as larvae that change shape and behavior as they grow. Some young reptiles have different-colored markings than their parents. After hatching, the little loggerheads dig out of their nest. They swarm out of the sand and streak for the sea. If it's too dark to see the waves, the baby loggerheads look for the nearest open horizon. The race to the waves is a dangerous time for them. Gulls and other seabirds—even raccoons—may catch them. As soon as they reach the water, the young turtles swim furiously, heading away from the beach to hide in seaweeds.

The female alligator makes a nest of vegetation and mud near water. She scoops up dirt, grass, reeds, twigs, and leaves in her huge jaws and puts it all in a pile, shaping it into a cone with her tail, sides, mouth, and feet. At times she leaves the pile and goes into the water. When she returns, dripping wet, she crawls back and forth on the pile, which is dampened by the water. Her weight also packs the pile down. It may take a female alligator two weeks to finish her nest, which is often about 2 feet (0.7 meter) high and 5 feet (2 meters) across.

When she is ready to lay eggs, the female alligator crawls on top of the nest. Her hind feet dig a hole, which she then straddles with her hind legs. Lifting her tail, she begins to lay eggs, dropping them into the hole, one by one. The eggs have whitish shells and an oblong shape and are about 3 inches (8 centimeters) long and 1 inch (2.5 centimeters) wide. All together, a female alligator may lay up to 60 eggs. When she is done, she covers the hole.

As the vegetation in the nest rots, it produces heat, which helps the embryos to grow. The nest also protects the eggs from severe temperature changes. Scientists who put a thermometer in one alligator nest found that the temperature inside the nest

DID YOU KNOW

The Lay Way

Not all reptiles are egg-layers. The blue-tongued skink of Australia and the Jackson's chameleon of Africa are two reptiles that give birth to live young—usually 5 to 25 at a time.

Two milk snakes emerge from their eggs. Young reptiles, unlike amphibians and fishes, look like miniature copies of their parents when they are born.

Reproduction and Growth

Feeling Skinny

Several days before a snake is ready to shed its skin, its physical appearance and behavior change drastically. Most often, its eyes become cloudy, its skin appears dull and colorless, it loses its appetite, and it becomes aggressive. Many snakes also seek out as much water as possible in anticipation of losing a great deal of body fluid when they lose their old skin.

averaged 83 degrees F. (28 degrees C.). Outside, the temperatures ranged from warm to cool.

Female alligators usually stay near their nests, and some—though not all—will defend them. For about two months, the alligator embryo lies curled in its egg, protected by a leathery shell. It is also protected by a tough lining under the shell. During the two months, the embryo feeds on the yolk of the egg. Eventually, the embryo becomes too large for the egg, and cracks begin to appear in the shell. Soon the shell breaks over the young alligator's head.

Before the alligator can get out of the egg, it must cut through the skin lining. On its snout there is a tooth-like bump, called the egg tooth, which the young alligator uses to cut out of the skin. Once its job has been done, the egg tooth disappears.

Getting out of the egg may take as long as a week. Once it is free, the young alligator is still deep inside the pile. If it has trouble digging its way out, the mother, responding to the baby's grunts, will tear mouthfuls of material from the pile. With the way clear, the young alligator then crawls out of the nest.

Gimme Some Skin

Molting garter snake

Most lizards and snakes regularly shed their skin in a process called molting, or sloughing. A reptile's dry, scaly exterior is made mostly out of a tough but flexible substance called keratin, which is similar to the substance that makes up human fingernails. The skin protects the animal's insides from the natural elements and from damage by predators. From time to time, a reptile's outer skin is shed and is replaced by fresh, new skin cells. This molting allows room for growth and also replaces worn-out or damaged skin.

Most lizards shed their skin in large flakes and often take a few days to slough all their old coating. Snakes, however, are able to slough their entire skin at one time, usually leaving it all in one piece and completing the process in about 30 minutes. For snakes, sloughing begins at the lips. Once sloughing has started, a snake rubs its head along the ground to peel its skin back. As it rubs, the snake turns the old skin inside out and crawls out of the old coating. Sloughing is a process that continues throughout a reptile's life because most reptiles never stop growing.

Gator Incubator

Alligators make their nests out of vegetation and mud and locate them near the water. When she is ready to lay her eggs, the female crawls on top of the nest and digs a hole with her hind feet. She then straddles the hole, deposits her eggs inside, and covers the hole. *Below, right:* After incubating in the warm nest, the young alligators are ready to emerge. Getting out of an egg may take as long as a week.

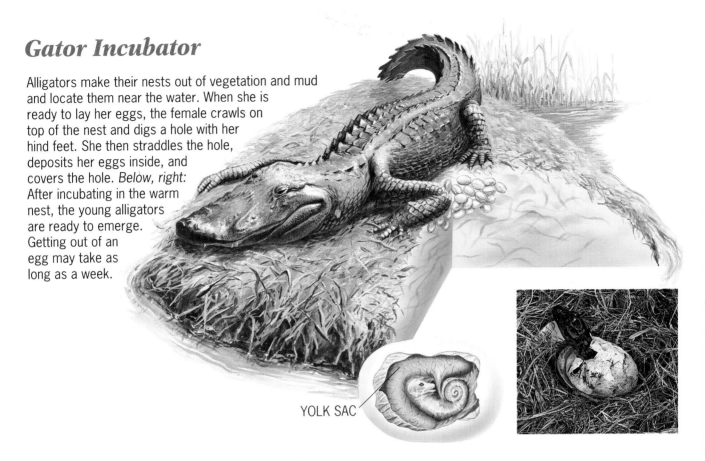

YOLK SAC

A baby alligator is about 8 inches (20 centimeters) long. Its hide is dark, like an adult's, but it has white markings. As an alligator grows, the markings turn yellow and eventually disappear. Scientists believe that the markings may be useful as camouflage and may also help older alligators recognize young ones.

Alligators grow very rapidly during their first five to eight years. The warmer its habitat, the faster a young alligator grows. Availability of food also speeds growth. Some young alligators add almost 18 inches (46 centimeters) to their length each year. An alligator will probably not grow any longer than 18 feet (5 meters)—most are smaller. A 12-foot (4-meter) long alligator is considered a big animal. After about five years, alligators begin to reproduce.

Alligators can live for a relatively long time. In captivity, they have lived more than 30 years. Many other reptiles also have very long life spans.

5

Fitting into the Web of Life

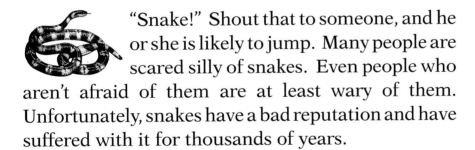 "Snake!" Shout that to someone, and he or she is likely to jump. Many people are scared silly of snakes. Even people who aren't afraid of them are at least wary of them. Unfortunately, snakes have a bad reputation and have suffered with it for thousands of years.

Not just snakes, but reptiles in general, have a reputation problem and have not been treated kindly by people. Perhaps that is because no other group of vertebrates is less understood by humans. Some people, for instance, wrongly believe that killing every snake they see helps the environment.

Reptiles have been hurt by all sorts of human activities. Human destruction of reptile habitats has probably been the most damaging. Such destruction is particularly harmful, since reptiles, like all other living things, play a significant role in the web of life and delicate balance of nature.

Opposite:
An alligator lies in its gator hole amid the thick vegetation of a swamp. Gator holes provide habitats for a variety of other living things, including plants and fish.

Helping Humans and Other Animals

Some snakes, such as venomous snakes, are certainly dangerous, but most snakes are not. And many of the venomous snakes can even be of help to people.

How can venomous snakes be helpful? It has to do with what they eat. Many snakes feed on animals that can be pests to humans: rodents—like rats and mice—and insects that destroy crops.

One gopher snake, 5 feet (2 meters) long, was found to have almost three dozen mice in its stomach. The snake lived on a farm in the western United States. Occasionally, farmers who are wise to the ways of snakes release species that will eat rodents and control the number of pests on their farms.

The American alligator plays a big role in shaping its environment and is another important reptile in the web of life. In Florida's Everglades, for instance, alligators often live in water-filled hollows called gator holes. Sometimes the alligators dig these holes, and other times they find a small pond and then keep it clear of vegetation.

Gator holes often provide a natural habitat for many other living things. Willow trees, for example, frequently grow around the rim of gator holes. These trees provide nesting sites for birds such as herons,

Snakes are helpful to humans in a variety of ways. Most important, snakes control the populations of rodents, insects, and other pests that can be troublesome to humans.

whose droppings fertilize the trees. Bass, sunfishes, frogs, and other water animals live in the gator holes. Herons, otters, and raccoons eat the frogs and fishes that the holes provide.

Gator holes are important when drought strikes the Everglades, causing most of this vast marsh and swamp to dry up. Since the gator holes are deep, they are a key source of water and food for Everglades wildlife during times of drought.

Partners in the Natural World

The relationship between reptiles and most other animals is usually one of predator and prey. Unlike most birds, insects, and fishes—which benefit from living in large groups—reptiles are mainly solitary creatures. Some reptiles do, however, live side by side with other animals in a sort of peaceful partnership. Lizards and snakes will frequently share a termite mound as an ideal place to incubate their eggs. The deep, cool burrow created by the gopher tortoise often hosts a number of other creatures, such as possums, rabbits, raccoons, and lizards—who live together successfully. Even rattlesnakes have been found inhabiting some tortoise burrows.

The African helmeted turtle is known to clean tiny parasites from large water-wading mammals such as the hippopotamus and the rhinoceros. Some turtles will even use their powerful jaws to clean ocean algae and other material off the shells of other turtles. When the cleaning turtle is done, it will often switch places with its partner in order to be cleaned.

Some reptiles rely even more directly on help and cooperation from other animals. The New Zealand tuatara depends a great deal on seabirds such as petrels and shearwaters for its existence. Sometimes it even shares its burrow with these birds. Most often

DID YOU KNOW

Snake-Offs and Landings

There is a snake in southern Asia that appears to fly through the air. The "flying" snake is an active hunter that hangs high up in the trees of thick forests and jumps from branch to branch in search of food. It can even glide through the air when it wants to reach lower levels. In order to slow down, the snake flattens its body to increase its surface and the resistance of the air.

Reptiles have many natural enemies, including other reptiles. Wild birds, such as hawks, owls, and herons, regularly prey on snakes and other small reptiles. Here, a red-tailed hawk eats a diamond-back rattlesnake.

the seabirds cover the rocks and ground near the burrow with droppings that attract and feed large numbers of insects, such as beetles and crickets. This, in turn, creates the perfect feeding ground for the tuatara, which happens to have a particular taste for these insects.

Some shore birds, such as the plover, have been known to clean scraps of food from the open mouths of crocodiles. The birds apparently enter the mouth of a sleeping crocodile and are allowed to pick safely while the reptile rests. The water dikkop, another aquatic bird, also makes good use of crocodiles. Dikkops often nest near crocodiles in order to be indirectly protected by them. Few predators will come near a dikkop's nest when a crocodile is nearby.

Natural Enemies

Snakes are eaten by many animals, including other snakes. The king cobra of southern Asia, the world's largest venomous snake, feeds almost entirely on other snakes. North American kingsnakes are not venomous—they are also snake-eaters that even eat rattlesnakes. Kingsnakes kill their prey the same way a boa constrictor does, by constriction that causes strangulation.

Chickens, turkeys, and ducks eat snakes that are young and small. Many wild birds, such as hawks, owls, and herons, regularly prey on snakes. Bears and raccoons will sometimes kill snakes, as will pigs—especially those pigs that run wild in the forest. Many predators of snakes also feed on lizards.

Defense in the Natural World

Most living things have natural enemies in their environments. To better survive, these organisms have developed unique adaptations that give them an advantage in certain situations. Reptiles have various adaptations that serve to protect them against danger. Some can run fast, some can hide themselves well, some use their tails as weapons, and others can fool enemies in various ways.

Running and hiding Most reptiles will defend themselves by running away, by hiding, or by running and hiding. Even venomous snakes prefer to get out of sight when they sense danger. Many small lizards are as fast as lightning—as soon as they sense trouble, they dash away.

Geckos are small lizards that live in the tropics and subtropics. Their toes have sharp claws, and most have pads under their toes that help them stick to surfaces. With its padded toes, a gecko can run straight up a wall or even upside down on a ceiling.

The flying lizard of southern Asia goes airborne to escape danger. It doesn't really fly, but it is a super glider. When it jumps from a tree, it extends flaps of skin on its sides that support it in the air. A flying lizard may glide up to 30 feet (9 meters) at once.

Reptiles have various adaptations that enable them to protect themselves in their environment. The double-crested basilisk lizard of Central America is also known as the Jesus Christ lizard because it can actually walk on water. When it is frightened, it will rear up on its hind legs and run away with remarkable speed. The basilisk can run either on land or across short stretches of water, using its incredible speed and long, thin toes to help support itself on the surface of a pond or stream.

The Mar-Shell Arts

The shell of a turtle protects it against enemies. The outer layer of the shell is made of hard, flat scales. Beneath the outer layer is a layer of thick bones. The upper half of the shell is supported by large, flat ribs that arch out from the backbone.

The bottom of the North American box turtle's shell is hinged with flaps. When the turtle draws its head, legs, and tail into the shell, the flaps on hinges close, and the turtle's body is completely boxed in.

Box turtle

In the deserts of the American Southwest lives the fringe-toed lizard. The animal's specially adapted toes hold it up when it runs across the sand and help it to move quickly by "swimming" away from its enemies by going under the sand.

A North American turtle called the stinkpot uses a defense that is much like a skunk's. When the stinkpot is frightened, glands on its thighs produce a foul smell that literally sends some predators running in the other direction.

Tail adaptations The spiny-tailed agamid lizard has a stout, strong tail that is covered with spines. When it is frightened, it scoots for its burrow and dives in, headfirst, with its tail sticking out of the burrow. If an enemy gets close enough, it will get smacked with the agamid's tail spines.

The small rubber boa has a round, blunt tail tip that resembles the boa's head. The boa uses this tail adaptation to fool enemies by coiling up into a ball with its head at the bottom of the coil. As its tail curls out of the top, enemies mistake the tail for the head and grab the wrong end of the boa.

The North American stinkpot turtle uses special odor glands on its thighs for defense. When it is frightened, the stinkpot produces a strong, foul smell that turns predators away.

Camouflage Natural camouflage, or blending in with the surroundings, helps an animal to hide in order to ambush prey. It also helps to hide an animal from creatures that threaten its life. Different reptiles have developed various ways of camouflaging themselves. The small European viper, which is the same color as sand, flattens itself into the sand and almost buries itself. Because of its natural disguise, this viper can make itself difficult for predators to see.

The alligator snapping turtle looks exactly like a stone when it lies motionless in the water. It often sits for hours, waiting for a possible meal to wander by. When its prey is close enough, the snapper ambushes it and snatches it into its powerful jaws.

Lizards, especially chameleons, are famous for their camouflage talents. Many types of lizards can alter the colors and patterns on their skin to blend perfectly with their surroundings. A chameleon's skin has several layers of color cells, or pigments. Changes in color or pattern on the skin are created when a dark-brown pigment is moved in and out of the upper layers of the skin. Many factors other than the physical surroundings can affect a lizard's color: changes in light levels, temperature changes, and the mood of a lizard. Often these changes occur very

DID YOU KNOW

Rattle-Tale

Do you know what makes a rattlesnake's tail rattle? The tip of the snake's tail is made up of hollow segments of keratin—the tough, flexible substance that makes up the skin. Each time a rattler sheds its skin, a new segment of keratin is added to its tail. The rattlesnake vibrates its tail as a warning to enemies, knocking the hollow segments of keratin together to make a rattling sound.

It's a Snap to Be a Turtle

Because of its ferocious appearance, the alligator snapping turtle was once believed to be half turtle and half alligator. Its very strong, knife-like jaws can chop most prey in half with a quick snap. Because its spiny back and bumpy legs make it look so much like a rock, the alligator snapper uses its deceiving appearance to catch food. When fishing for prey, the turtle lies motionless on the bottom of a river or pond with its mouth wide open. Inside its mouth, at the end of its tongue, is a remarkable worm-like appendage that fills with blood and looks just like an earthworm. As the turtle sits motionless, it wiggles its "worm" to attract fish and other animals of prey. When the prey arrives and goes after the bait, the turtle snaps its powerful jaws closed and enjoys a meal.

Alligator snapping turtle

Chameleons are masters of disguise. In a fraction of a second, a chameleon can change its color by rearranging the color cells in its skin. Here, a chameleon transforms itself from yellow (*left*) to green (*right*) almost instantly.

DID YOU KNOW

Lil' Squirts

The horned lizard (sometimes called the horned toad) of the American West has an unusual method of self-defense. It can squirt a stream of blood at its enemies. The blood actually comes from veins in the lizard's eyes, and the stream can reach up to 7 feet (2 meters) away!

fast. An anole lizard can change its appearance from brown to green in a matter of seconds. Once the anole's color matches its surroundings, it is very difficult for another animal to see it.

Bluffing Bluffing an enemy is another way some reptiles avoid being eaten. By acting bigger or more dangerous than they really are, bluffers can often scare enemies away. The rat snake is not venomous, but when it is threatened, it acts a little bit like a dangerous rattlesnake. It coils up, hissing loudly, and its tail vibrates. In dead leaves, the tail can make a buzzing sound that is similar to the rattling of a rattlesnake.

The frilled lizard of Australia is about 8 inches (20 centimeters) long. Around its head is a ruff of skin. Normally, the lizard keeps the ruff flat, but when it is frightened, it raises the front of its body high off the ground. Its big mouth opens wide, and the ruff spreads out, becoming as wide as the lizard is long. This sudden, ferocious movement makes the lizard seem much bigger and more dangerous than it is and is very effective at startling an enemy.

The hognose snake bluffs enemies in two ways. First it tries to frighten them by coiling and puffing up its body. Then it opens its mouth and hisses. If this drama doesn't work, the hognose snake flops over on

its back, mouth open, and plays dead. The hognose, however, is not always completely believable. If you turn a "dead" hognose snake on its belly, it will roll over onto its back again.

Reptiles and Humans: Together in the Natural World

The Earth was at one time ruled by reptiles. The situation is very different today, however. Nearly 150 million years later, only four major groups of reptiles remain. Destructive human activities on our planet are mostly responsible for this serious and growing problem. Tropical rain forests in Brazil and Central America are home to thousands of species of reptiles. But these habitats are quickly disappearing as pollution and commercial development destroy critical food sources and shelter for hundreds of thousands of plants and animals.

Many people are not sympathetic to the loss of reptile populations. Ignorance about reptiles has traditionally made people fearful of them. It has also made it difficult to get support for their cause. Unlike pandas or baby gorillas—which are considered "cute" and "cuddly"—reptiles are viewed as "cold" and "slimy" by most who don't know them. These people forget that every living thing in the natural world has a unique and irreplaceable beauty all its own.

Humans and reptiles interact in a number of ways. While reptiles are not as popular as dogs or cats, snakes, lizards, and turtles are common pets. Conservationists suggest, however, that people do not make pets out of reptiles that are rare in the wild. Some reptiles are protected by laws that prohibit people from removing them from their natural habitats. Still, many reptiles, such as boa constrictors, are bred in captivity for the pet trade.

The frilled lizard of Australia (*top*) raises the front of its body and spreads out its wide ruff when it is threatened. The hognose snake (*bottom*) flips over on its back and plays dead to fool its enemies.

DID YOU KNOW

Getting the Tail End

Tuataras and many lizards, such as skinks, actually have detachable tails. When an enemy grabs one of them by the tail, the tail breaks off. The enemy is then left with only a tail as the animal runs away. Later the reptile grows a new tail.

Choose Your Poison: Venomous Reptiles

Of the approximately 3,000 kinds of snakes in existence, only about 200 are venomous. Of the 3,000 kinds of lizards, only 2 are poisonous. Venomous snakes have a bad reputation with humans. Because they are dangerous, many people fear these reptiles and think of them as "evil." But venomous snakes do not intend to be mean or nasty. They are just using the special adaptations they have developed in order to survive in the natural world.

A snake injects venom into its victim through its hollow fangs, which are attached to the glands that produce the poison. Different snakes produce different kinds of venom. Some of the most venomous snakes are sea snakes, which can swim extremely fast and can stay underwater for up to five hours. The venom of most snakes is usually powerful enough to slow or stun prey long enough to kill them. Some venom is so powerful that it can kill large animals in a matter of seconds.

Viper being milked for venom

About 30,000 people are bitten each year by venomous snakes. Most snake-bite victims live in tropical countries, where venomous snakes are common and where people often walk barefoot. Very few people, however, die each year from snakebites. Most deaths could be prevented with a medicine that counter-acts the poison, but in many developing countries medicines are not available. Snake venom is actually used in the production of anti-snakebite medicines called serums. Many serum producers will milk snakes for their venom by holding the head and squeezing the venom sac. The venom is then added to a fluid that is designed to block the effects of snake poison in the body.

Poisonous snakes are found in many parts of the world and in almost every kind of habitat. Tropical areas, however, seem to have more venomous snakes than other places. The two poisonous lizards—the Gila monster and the Mexican beaded lizard—are both found in the southwestern United States. The following is a brief listing of some common poisonous snakes with their average size, the characteristics of their venom, and the areas they generally inhabit.

Boomslang

The hides of many reptiles are used by humans to create clothing, footwear, and other accessories. Some reptiles, such as certain pythons, are rapidly decreasing in number because they have been overhunted for their skins, which are frequently used for boots. Conservationists therefore try to discourage people from buying snakeskin boots. Using reptile products is not always harmful to wildlife conservation efforts. Crocodiles are farmed in some developing countries for hides that are made into shoes, belts, and similar items. Some of the money earned from the sale of the

AFRICA

Boomslang (4–6.5 feet/1–2 meters): Venom attacks blood cells and prevents clotting.

African twig snake (4–6 feet/1–2 meters): Venom is similar to that of the boomslang.

Black mamba (6.5–14 feet/2–4 meters): Longest venomous snake in Africa; potent venom that attacks the brain and the heart.

ASIA

King cobra (8–18 feet/2–5 meters): World's largest venomous snake; venom is extremely toxic to humans.

AUSTRALIA

Death adder (16–40 inches/41–102 centimeters): One of the world's most deadly snakes; venom is extremely strong.

EUROPE

Adder (20–35 inches/51–89 centimeters): Commonly considered one of the least aggressive and least dangerous of the venomous snakes.

NORTH AMERICA

Copperhead (22–53 inches/56–135 centimeters): Bites are painful but not considered very dangerous to humans.

Eastern diamondback rattlesnake (3–8 feet/1–2 meters): Largest and most dangerous snake in the United States; deadly venom that works quickly.

Western diamondback rattlesnake (3–7 feet/1–2 meters): Like its eastern relative, one of the largest and most dangerous snakes in North America; responsible for more serious snakebites and deaths than any other North American serpent.

King cobra

Western diamondback rattlesnake

hides is put back into conserving crocodiles in the wild. Several years ago, when alligators were endangered, it was illegal to hunt them or sell their hides. Today, the alligator population has recovered and, in some parts of the United States, alligators are too numerous for their habitats. In these places, a small number of alligators can now be hunted, and their hides and meat can be legally marketed.

Reptiles that are farmed for commercial purposes can provide food for people. In some areas of the American Southwest, it is not uncommon to find

DID YOU KNOW

A Lot of Hot Air

When a chuckwalla is threatened, it often creeps into a crevice in the rocks and then fills its fat body full of air. This way, the chuckwalla is wedged into the crevice. It is very difficult for a predator to dislodge a blown-up chuckwalla in a crevice.

Amazing Shell Life

You may have heard that some turtles live for hundreds of years. That's not exactly true, but turtles can reach an amazing age. Many have the ability to live more than 100 years, but in nature only a few do. In captivity, some giant tortoises of the Galápagos Islands have lived more than 100 years. One box turtle is known to have lived more than 123 years.

The giant tortoise of the Galápagos Islands in the Pacific became an endangered species because of the activities of humans.

rattlesnake chili on a menu, and in parts of Florida, alligator is used in local dishes. Restaurants in the Caribbean and Asia serve turtle soup, but in many cases the turtles have been hunted illegally, which threatens the survival of certain species.

Endangered Reptiles

A number of reptiles in various parts of the world are considered endangered species. Land development threatens the loggerhead turtle in Turkey, one of the last breeding grounds for the reptile. The giant skink of the Solomon Islands is also suffering from the rapid loss of its natural habitat.

On the Galápagos Islands in the Pacific live huge land tortoises that can weigh more than 250 pounds (113 kilograms). Fifteen different kinds of Galápagos tortoises were once spread throughout the islands, and each kind developed a shell that had a different shape. One, for instance, was dome-shaped. Another looked like a saddle.

When Europeans arrived on the islands about 500 years ago, the tortoises began to dwindle. Sailors killed the big, slow reptiles for food, and the rats that came to the Galápagos on European ships ate tortoise eggs. European goats also ate down vegetation, which served as food for tortoises.

Today, only 10 kinds of tortoises remain, and none are common. Humans originally endangered the Galápagos tortoises, but now they are working to save them (tortoises are presently protected by law). More and more, people around the world are realizing that reptiles are marvelous animals with important roles to play in nature. They are different from us, yet humans, reptiles, and all other living things share similar characteristics. They also share the most precious thing of all—our fragile, beautiful planet.

Classification Chart of Reptiles

Kingdom: Animal
Phylum: Chordata
Class: Reptilia

Scientists have identified about 6,200 species of reptiles. These species are classified into four orders (different scientists use different classification systems).

Major Order	Common Members	Distinctive Features
Chelonia	turtles	box-like shell; ability to withdraw head, usually into shell
Crocodilia	alligators, crocodiles, gavials, caimans	armored skin; teeth in sockets; very good hearing
Squamata	lizards, snakes	Jacobson's organ; paired male sex organ; snakes are limbless
Rhynchocephalia	tuataras	eye-like organ in middle of head; crest on back and tail

THE ANIMAL KINGDOM

Porifera SPONGES

Cnidaria COELENTERATES

Platyhelminthes FLATWORMS

Nematoda ROUNDWORMS

Mollusca MOLLUSKS

Annelida TRUE WORMS

Hydrozoa HYDRAS, HYDROIDS

Scyphozoa JELLYFISH

Anthozoa SEA ANEMONES, CORALS

Turbellaria FREE-LIVING FLATWORMS

Monogenea PARASITIC FLUKES

Trematoda PARASITIC FLUKES

Cestoda TAPEWORMS

Polyplacophora CHITONS

Gastropoda SNAILS, SLUGS

Bivalvia CLAMS, SCALLOPS MUSSELS

Cephalopoda OCTOPUSES, SQUID

Polychaeta MARINE WORMS

Oligochaeta EARTHWORMS, FRESHWATER WORMS

Hirudinea LEECHES

Biological Classification

The branch of biology that deals with classification is called taxonomy, or systematics. Biological classification is the arrangement of living organisms into categories. Biologists have created a universal system of classification that they can share with one another, no matter where they study or what language they speak. The categories in a classification chart are based on the natural similarities of the organisms. The similarities considered are the structure of the organism, the development (reproduction and growth), biochemical and physiological functions (metabolism and senses), and evolutionary history. Biologists classify living things to show relationships between different groups of organisms, both ancient and modern. Classification charts are also useful in tracing the evolutionary pathways along which present-day organisms have evolved.

Over the years, the classification process has been altered as new information has become accepted. A long time ago, biologists used a two-kingdom system of classification; every living thing was considered a member of either the plant kingdom or the animal kingdom. Today, many biologists use a five-kingdom system that includes plants, animals, monera (microbes), protista (protozoa and certain molds), and fungi (non-green plants). In every kingdom, however, the hierarchy of classification remains the same. In this chart, groupings go from the most general categories (at the top) down to groups that are more and more specific. The most general grouping is PHYLUM. The most specific is ORDER. To use the chart, you may want to find the familiar name of an organism in a CLASS or ORDER box and then trace its classification upward until you reach its PHYLUM.

Insecta INSECTS

Chilopoda CENTIPEDES

Diplopoda MILLIPEDES

Symphyla, Pauropoda SYMPHYLANS, PAUROPODS

Collembola, SPRINGTAILS
Thysanura, SILVERFISH, BRISTLETAILS
Ephemeroptera, MAYFLIES
Odonata, DRAGONFLIES, DAMSELFLIES
Isoptera, TERMITES
Orthoptera, LOCUSTS, CRICKETS, GRASSHOPPERS
Dictyptera, COCKROACHES, MANTIDS
Dermaptera, EARWIGS
Phasmida, STICK INSECTS, LEAF INSECTS
Psocoptera, BOOK LICE, BARK LICE
Diplura, SIMPLE INSECTS
Protura, TELSONTAILS
Plecoptera, STONEFLIES
Grylloblattodea, TINY MOUNTAIN INSECTS
Strepsiptera, TWISTED-WINGED STYLOPIDS
Trichoptera, CADDIS FLIES

Embioptera, WEBSPINNERS
Thysanoptera, THRIPS
Mecoptera, SCORPION FLIES
Zoraptera, RARE TROPICAL INSECTS
Hemiptera, TRUE BUGS
Anoplura, SUCKING LICE
Mallophaga, BITING LICE, BIRD LICE
Homoptera, WHITE FLIES, APHIDS, SCALE INSECTS, CICADAS
Coleoptera, BEETLES, WEEVILS
Neuroptera, ALDERFLIES, LACEWINGS, ANT LIONS, SNAKE FLIES, DOBSONFLIES
Hymenoptera, ANTS, BEES, WASPS
Siphonaptera, FLEAS
Diptera, TRUE FLIES, MOSQUITOES, GNATS
Lepidoptera, BUTTERFLIES, MOTHS

Insectivora, INSECTIVORES (e.g., shrews, moles, hedgehogs)
Chiroptera, BATS
Dermoptera, FLYING LEMURS
Edentata, ANTEATERS, SLOTHS, ARMADILLOS
Pholidota, PANGOLINS
Primates, PROSIMIANS (e.g., lemurs, tarsiers, monkeys, apes, humans)
Rodentia, RODENTS (e.g., squirrels, rats, beavers, mice, porcupines)
Lagomorpha, RABBITS, HARES, PIKAS
Cetacea, WHALES, DOLPHINS, PORPOISES

Carnivora, CARNIVORES (e.g., cats, dogs, weasels, bears, hyenas)
Pinnipedia, SEALS, SEA LIONS, WALRUSES
Tubulidentata, AARDVARKS
Hyracoidea, HYRAXES
Proboscidea, ELEPHANTS
Sirenia, SEA COWS (e.g., manatees, dugongs)
Perissodactyla, ODD-TOED HOOFED MAMMALS (e.g., horses, rhinoceroses, tapirs)
Artiodactyla, EVEN-TOED HOOFED MAMMALS (e.g., hogs, cattle, camels, hippopotamuses)

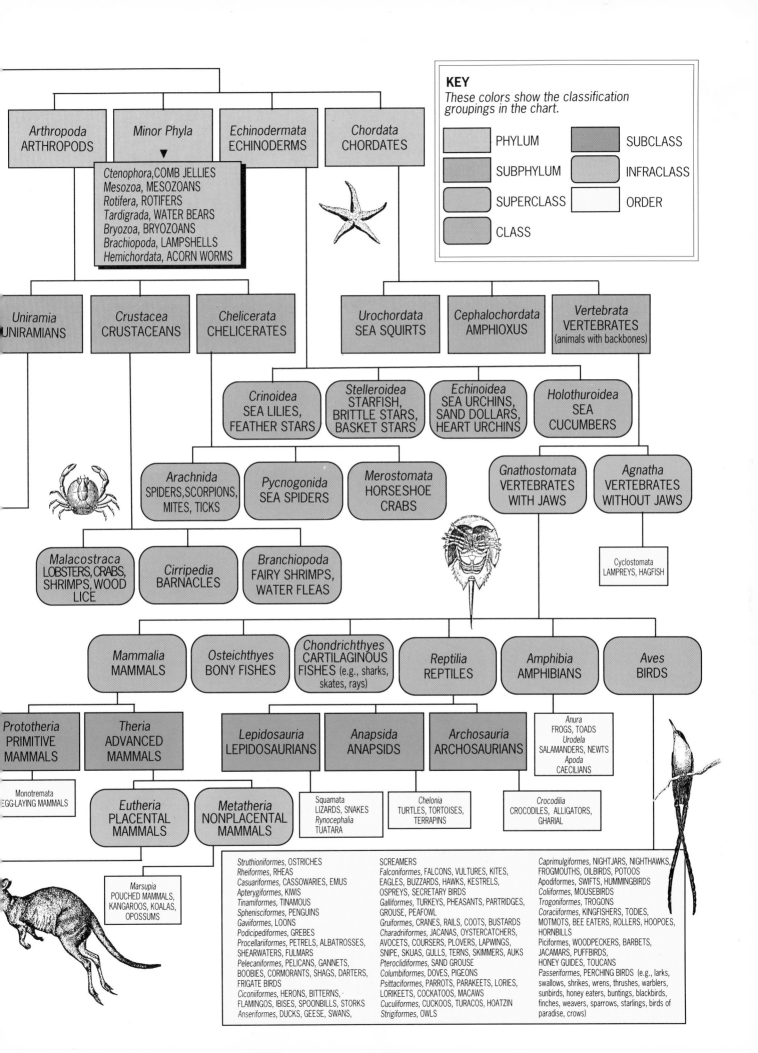

KEY
These colors show the classification groupings in the chart.

PHYLUM · SUBCLASS · SUBPHYLUM · INFRACLASS · SUPERCLASS · ORDER · CLASS

Arthropoda ARTHROPODS

Minor Phyla ▼
Ctenophora, COMB JELLIES
Mesozoa, MESOZOANS
Rotifera, ROTIFERS
Tardigrada, WATER BEARS
Bryozoa, BRYOZOANS
Brachiopoda, LAMPSHELLS
Hemichordata, ACORN WORMS

Echinodermata ECHINODERMS

Chordata CHORDATES

Uniramia UNIRAMIANS

Crustacea CRUSTACEANS

Chelicerata CHELICERATES

Urochordata SEA SQUIRTS

Cephalochordata AMPHIOXUS

Vertebrata VERTEBRATES (animals with backbones)

Crinoidea SEA LILIES, FEATHER STARS

Stelleroidea STARFISH, BRITTLE STARS, BASKET STARS

Echinoidea SEA URCHINS, SAND DOLLARS, HEART URCHINS

Holothuroidea SEA CUCUMBERS

Arachnida SPIDERS, SCORPIONS, MITES, TICKS

Pycnogonida SEA SPIDERS

Merostomata HORSESHOE CRABS

Gnathostomata VERTEBRATES WITH JAWS

Agnatha VERTEBRATES WITHOUT JAWS

Malacostraca LOBSTERS, CRABS, SHRIMPS, WOOD LICE

Cirripedia BARNACLES

Branchiopoda FAIRY SHRIMPS, WATER FLEAS

Cyclostomata LAMPREYS, HAGFISH

Mammalia MAMMALS

Osteichthyes BONY FISHES

Chondrichthyes CARTILAGINOUS FISHES (e.g., sharks, skates, rays)

Reptilia REPTILES

Amphibia AMPHIBIANS

Aves BIRDS

Prototheria PRIMITIVE MAMMALS

Theria ADVANCED MAMMALS

Lepidosauria LEPIDOSAURIANS

Anapsida ANAPSIDS

Archosauria ARCHOSAURIANS

Anura FROGS, TOADS
Urodela SALAMANDERS, NEWTS
Apoda CAECILIANS

Monotremata EGG-LAYING MAMMALS

Eutheria PLACENTAL MAMMALS

Metatheria NONPLACENTAL MAMMALS

Squamata LIZARDS, SNAKES
Rynocephalia TUATARA

Chelonia TURTLES, TORTOISES, TERRAPINS

Crocodilia CROCODILES, ALLIGATORS, GHARIAL

Marsupia POUCHED MAMMALS, KANGAROOS, KOALAS, OPOSSUMS

Struthioniformes, OSTRICHES
Rheiformes, RHEAS
Casuariformes, CASSOWARIES, EMUS
Apterygiformes, KIWIS
Tinamiformes, TINAMOUS
Sphenisciformes, PENGUINS
Gaviiformes, LOONS
Podicipediformes, GREBES
Procellariiformes, PETRELS, ALBATROSSES, SHEARWATERS, FULMARS
Pelecaniformes, PELICANS, GANNETS, BOOBIES, CORMORANTS, SHAGS, DARTERS, FRIGATE BIRDS
Ciconiiformes, HERONS, BITTERNS, FLAMINGOS, IBISES, SPOONBILLS, STORKS
Anseriformes, DUCKS, GEESE, SWANS,

SCREAMERS
Falconiformes, FALCONS, VULTURES, KITES, EAGLES, BUZZARDS, HAWKS, KESTRELS, OSPREYS, SECRETARY BIRDS
Galliformes, TURKEYS, PHEASANTS, PARTRIDGES, GROUSE, PEAFOWL
Gruiformes, CRANES, RAILS, COOTS, BUSTARDS
Charadriiformes, JACANAS, OYSTERCATCHERS, AVOCETS, COURSERS, PLOVERS, LAPWINGS, SNIPE, SKUAS, GULLS, TERNS, SKIMMERS, AUKS
Pteroclidiformes, SAND GROUSE
Columbiformes, DOVES, PIGEONS
Psittaciformes, PARROTS, PARAKEETS, LORIES, LORIKEETS, COCKATOOS, MACAWS
Cuculiformes, CUCKOOS, TURACOS, HOATZIN
Strigiformes, OWLS

Caprimulgiformes, NIGHTJARS, NIGHTHAWKS, FROGMOUTHS, OILBIRDS, POTOOS
Apodiformes, SWIFTS, HUMMINGBIRDS
Coliiformes, MOUSEBIRDS
Trogoniformes, TROGONS
Coraciiformes, KINGFISHERS, TODIES, MOTMOTS, BEE EATERS, ROLLERS, HOOPOES, HORNBILLS
Piciformes, WOODPECKERS, BARBETS, JACAMARS, PUFFBIRDS, HONEY GUIDES, TOUCANS
Passeriformes, PERCHING BIRDS (e.g., larks, swallows, shrikes, wrens, thrushes, warblers, sunbirds, honey eaters, buntings, blackbirds, finches, weavers, sparrows, starlings, birds of paradise, crows)

Glossary

adaptation A body part or behavior that helps an organism survive in its environment.

amoeba A type of one-celled organism.

articular One of the two bones in a reptile's jaw joint.

atrium An upper chamber of the heart, through which blood flows to a ventricle.

binocular vision Using both eyes to see in three dimensions.

camouflage The colors, shapes, behaviors, or structures that enable an organism to blend with its surroundings.

cloaca The structure on a reptile where the digestive, urinary, and reproductive systems open.

cones Light-sensitive cells in the eye that are most sensitive in bright light and register color.

digestion The mechanical and chemical breakdown of food into substances the body can use for growth and energy.

embryo A young developing organism.

enzyme A substance that breaks down food throughout the digestive system.

evolve To change over a long period of time.

extinct No longer in existence.

fertilize To join a sperm with an egg to create a new organism.

habitat The particular part of the environment in which an organism lives.

hibernation A seasonal period of rest when the body processes slow down.

hormones Chemicals that regulate body processes.

iris A covering for the lens of the eye that channels light to the lens.

Jacobson's organ A sensory organ above the roof of the mouth in snakes and lizards.

keratin A hard substance found in the skin, hair, nails, claws, feathers, hooves, scales, and horns of animals.

lens A clear structure at the center of the eye through which light passes to the retina.

metabolism The chemical processes in cells that are essential to life.

molecule The smallest particle of a substance that retains all the properties of the substance.

nictitating membrane The third "eyelid" of a reptile, which keeps the eyes protected.

optic nerve One of a pair of nerves that send visual stimuli to the brain.

poacher A person who takes wildlife illegally.

predator An animal that kills other animals.

prey Animals that are eaten by other animals.

quadrate One of the two bones in a reptile's jaw joint.

reproduction The process by which organisms create other members of their species.

retina A light-sensitive coating on the back of the eye, like the film of a camera.

rods Light-sensitive cells in the back of the eye that are most sensitive in dim light and register only black and white.

scutes The bony scales of crocodilians.

sensory nerves Nerves that carry messages from the sense organs to the brain.

species A group of organisms that share many traits with one another and that can reproduce with one another.

sperm The male reproductive cell that fertilizes a female egg.

stapes The bone behind the eardrum through which vibrations are transmitted.

stimuli Messages from the surroundings that are detected by an organism.

tapetum A layer of cells behind the retina of an alligator's eye that allows the alligator to see better at night.

venom Poison.

ventricle A chamber within a vertebrate's heart that pumps blood.

vertebrae The bones that make up the backbone.

vertebrate An animal with a backbone.

For Further Reading

Bender, Lionel. *First Sight: Lizards & Dragons*. New York: Franklin Watts, 1990.

Bender, Lionel. *Fish to Reptiles*. New York: Franklin Watts, 1988.

Berger, Melvin. *Dinosaurs*. New York: Avon, 1990.

Cohen, Daniel, and Cohen, Susan. *Where to Find Dinosaurs Today*. New York: Dutton, 1992.

Conant, Roger. *Peterson First Guide to Reptiles & Amphibians*. Boston: Houghton Mifflin, 1992.

Dow, Lesley. *Alligators & Crocodiles*. New York: Facts On File, 1990.

Gravelle, Karen. *Lizards*. New York: Franklin Watts, 1991.

Illustrated Encyclopedia of Wildlife, Vol. 9: *Reptiles and Amphibians*. Lakeville, CT: Grey Castle, 1990.

Losito, Linda. *Reptiles & Amphibians*. New York: Facts On File, 1989.

Massare, Judy A. *Prehistoric Marine Reptiles: Sea Monsters During the Age of Dinosaurs*. New York: Franklin Watts, 1991.

McCarthy, Colin. *First Sight: Poisonous Snakes*. New York: Franklin Watts, 1987.

McCarthy, Colin, and Arnold, Nick. *Reptile*. New York: Alfred A. Knopf, 1991.

Peissel, Michael, and Allen, Missy. *Dangerous Reptilian Creatures*. New York: Chelsea House, 1993.

Pettit, Jayne. *Amazing Lizards*. New York: Scholastic, 1990.

Sanford, William R., and Green, Carl R. *The Boa Constrictor*. New York: Macmillan, 1987.

Steele, Philip. *Extinct Reptiles: And Those in Danger of Extinction*. New York: Franklin Watts, 1991.

Tesar, Jenny. *Endangered Habitats*. New York: Facts On File, 1991.

Tesar, Jenny. *Shrinking Forests*. New York: Facts On File, 1991.

White, William. *All About the Turtle*. New York: Sterling, 1992.

Index

Photo Credits
Cover and title page: ©Kenneth W. Fink/Photo Researchers, Inc.; p. 6: ©F. Gohier/Photo Researchers, Inc.; p. 8: ©Jany Sauvanet/Photo Researchers, Inc.; p. 9: ©Tom McHugh/Photo Researchers, Inc. (left), ©Tom McHugh/Atlanta Zoo/Photo Researchers, Inc. (middle), ©David Norris/Photo Researchers, Inc. (right); p. 13: ©Tom McHugh/Steinhart Aquarium/Photo Researchers, Inc.; p. 14: ©Jeff Lepore/Photo Researchers, Inc.; p. 16: ©Stephen Dalton/Photo Researchers, Inc.; p. 18: ©Stephen Dalton/Photo Researchers, Inc.; p. 20: ©Gregory G. Dimijian/Photo Researchers, Inc. (top), ©Jeff Lepore/Photo Researchers, Inc. (bottom); p. 21: ©Karl Weidmann/Photo Researchers, Inc. (top), ©Joseph T. Collins/Photo Researchers, Inc. (bottom); p. 22: ©Jeff Lepore/Photo Researchers, Inc.; p. 23: ©Robert J. Erwin/Photo Researchers, Inc.; p. 24: ©Tom McHugh/Photo Researchers, Inc.; p. 26: ©Tom McHugh/Steinhart Aquarium/Photo Researchers, Inc.; p. 28: ©Tom McHugh/Photo Researchers, Inc.; p. 29: ©George Kleiman/Photo Researchers, Inc.; p. 30: ©Jany Sauvanet/Photo Researchers, Inc.; p. 31: ©Tom McHugh/Photo Researchers, Inc.; p. 32: ©Tom McHugh/Photo Researchers, Inc.; p. 36: ©Francois Gohier/Photo Researchers, Inc.; p. 39: ©J. H. Robinson/Photo Researchers, Inc.; p. 40: ©M. Reardon/Photo Researchers, Inc.; p. 41: ©Scott Camazine/Photo Researchers, Inc.; p. 42: ©Cosmos Blank/NAS/Photo Researchers, Inc.; p. 43: ©Dr. Robt. Potts, Jr./Photo Researchers, Inc.; p. 44: ©Stephen J. Krasemann/Photo Researchers, Inc.; p. 46: ©Craig K. Lorenz/Photo Researchers, Inc.; p. 48: ©Len Rue, Jr./Photo Researchers, Inc.; p. 49: ©Stephen Dalton/Photo Researchers, Inc.; p. 50: ©Jeff Lepore/Photo Researchers, Inc. (top), ©Tom McHugh/Steinhart Aquarium/Photo Researchers, Inc. (bottom); p. 51: ©Cosmos Blank/Photo Researchers, Inc.; p. 52: ©Nuridsany et Pérennou/Photo Researchers, Inc.; p. 53: ©John Cancalosi/OKAPIA/Photo Researchers, Inc. (top), ©Larry Miller/Photo Researchers, Inc. (bottom); p. 54: ©John Bennett Dobbins/Photo Researchers, Inc. (top), ©M. Reardon/Photo Researchers, Inc. (bottom); p. 55: ©R. Van Nostrand/Photo Researchers, Inc. (top), ©Stephen Dalton/Photo Researchers, Inc. (bottom); p. 56: ©Francois Gohier/Photo Researchers, Inc.

Technical illustrations: ©Blackbirch Press, Inc.

4